OWLS

Rourke Enterprises, Inc.
Vero Beach, Florida 32964

PHOTO CREDITS

© Dwight R. Kuhn/DRK Photo: Page 13;
© Lynn M. Stone: all other photos.

ACKNOWLEDGMENTS

The author wishes to thank the following for
photographic assistance in the preparation of this
book: Chicago Zoological Society (Brookfield Zoo);
Alpenzoo, Vienna, Austria

Library of Congress Cataloging-in-Publication Data

Stone, Lynn M.
  Owls / by Lynn M. Stone

    p. cm. — (Bird discovery library)
    Includes index.
    Summary: Describes the appearance, habits, daily life, nesting,
infancy, and enemies of this nocturnal bird.
    ISBN 0-86592-326-4
    1. Owls—Juvenile literature. [1. Owls.] I. Title.
II. Series: Stone, Lynn M. Bird discovery library.
QL696.S8S748 1989   ˙ 88-31602
598'.97 - dc19   CIP
                                            AC

TABLE OF CONTENTS

OWLS

You are more likely to hear an owl than to see one. Most owls fly late in the day, early in the morning, or at night. They are difficult to see.

Owls are easy to hear. Eighteen **species,** or kinds, of owls live in the United States and Canada. All are noisy. They hoot, hiss, snore, whinny, scream, and make many other sounds. The barred owl *(Strix varia)* calls from the woods, "Who cooks for you? Who cooks for you all?"

About 130 species of owls live throughout the world. Most of them are **nocturnal,** which means they are active during the night. The owl's ability to fly and hunt at night make it one of the world's most unusual birds.

Great Horned Owl

WHERE THEY LIVE

Owls live on every continent except Antarctica. Many species live in forests or along forest edges. For those owls, the forest is their home or **habitat.** The snowy owl *(Nyctea scandiaca)* lives on the nearly treeless Arctic tundra. Other owls live in rain forests, deserts, and on prairies.

The best-known owl in North America, the great horned *(Bubo virginianus),* lives in many habitats. It can be found in all 50 American states, Canada, Mexico, and throughout South America.

Some owls **migrate** from one home to another. They fly south when food becomes scarce.

Barred Owl *(Strix varia)*

HOW THEY LOOK

Owls have sharp **talons** for toes and short, hooked beaks like hawks. Owls, however, are different from hawks in many ways.

Owls have large, round heads and big, bright eyes that face forward like ours. A hawk's eyes are on the sides of its head.

Most owls have short tails and long, broad wings. Their **plumage,** the covering of feathers, is usually a mix of gray, tan, and brown. Males and females are colored alike, but females are larger than males.

The smallest American owl is the elf owl *(Micrathene whitneyi),* just five inches long. The great gray owl *(Strix nebulosa)* is the longest at 33 inches.

"Ear" Tuft

Eye

Ear (Hidden)

Hooked
Beak

THE OWL'S EYES AND EARS

The eyes and ears of owls are remarkable. Barn owls and other nocturnal species can see in almost total darkness. Owls see well in daylight, too, but most species of owls find it easier to hunt at night. In darkness they can surprise their **prey,** the animals they hunt.

Owl ears are as keen as owl eyes. They can hear a mouse squeak or the rustle of an animal on leaves.

The great horned owl, the little screech owl *(Otus asio),* and several other owls have head feathers that look like cat ears. These ear tufts have nothing to do with the owl's real ears, which are hidden.

Screech Owl *(Otus asio)*   11

Barn Owl *(Tyto alba)*

Saw-whet Owl
(*Aegolius acadicus*)

THE OWL'S DAY

Owls are **predators.** They kill other animals for food. All owls spend some of their day—or night—hunting. Nocturnal owls loaf during the bright hours. They perch in trees, nap, hoot back and forth, and clean their feathers. Often they put up with attacks by pesky mobs of little birds.

A few owls hunt by day and rest at night. The snowy, pygmy *(Glaucidium gnoma),* ferruginous *(Glaucidium brasilianum),* and hawk *(Surnia ulula)* owls are daylight hunters.

Some owls, such as the burrowing owl *(Athene cunicularia),* may hunt day or night.

Snowy Owl *(Nyctea scandiaca)*

OWL NESTS

The great horned owl doesn't build a nest. It takes over the nest of a hawk, eagle, or crow.

The snowy owl and short-eared owl *(Asio flammeus)* nest on the ground. Burrowing owls nest in holes in the ground.

Most owls nest in holes in trees. They add a few feathers or sticks, but owls are not true nest builders.

No owl defends its nest more fiercely than the great horned owl. It will attack hawks, other owls, and even people. One man who was clawed by a great horned owl's talons thought he was being scalped. No wonder the great horned owl is nicknamed the ''winged tiger.''

Burrowing Owl
(Athene cunicularia)

BABY OWLS

Most tree-nesting owls lay two white eggs. Ground-nesting owls may lay a dozen eggs.

Female owls sit on the eggs to keep them warm. Male owls hunt and bring food to the nest.

The eggs in an owl's tree nest hatch at different times. If food is plentiful, the younger baby may survive. Otherwise, the youngest bird in the nest dies because the larger baby takes the food.

Baby owls—owlets—stay in the nest for several weeks. Their soft, fuzzy baby feathers are slowly replaced by adult feathers. Great horned owls begin flying when they are about 65 days old.

PREY

Owls often hunt at night in the same area a hawk hunted by day. Darkness is no problem for the owl. Owl feathers are soft and fluffy so that the owl can fly silently. He can listen for his prey. He flies more slowly than a hawk, but his quiet flight catches his prey by surprise.

Owls eat all kinds of small animals—mice, rats, birds, rabbits, snakes, insects, skunks, crabs, fish. Most owls eat their prey whole—bones, beaks, feet, and feathers.

Hawks tear their prey to pieces. Hawks bring their beaks down to their talons to eat. Owls lift their prey up to their beaks.

Screech Owl with Mouse

OWLS AND PEOPLE

People have always been interested in owls. Owls are a part of many legends. American Indians are especially fond of tales about owls. The Greeks of many hundreds of years ago thought owls were wise.

Today people know that owls are not wiser than other birds. But people are very fond of owls.

In America, owls are protected by law. People enjoy watching and listening to them. People help save owls in centers for injured **birds of prey**—hawks, eagles, and owls.

Hearing the calls of owls is one of the joys of being in the woods. If we protect these owl homes, we'll have owls for many years to come.

GLOSSARY

Birds of prey (BIRDS uhv pray)—birds with talons and hooked beaks which feed on other animals

Habitat (HAB a tat)—an animals home surroundings, such as the forest

Migrate (MY grate)—to move or fly from one place to another at the same time each year.

Nocturnal (nok TUR nal)—those animals more active at night than in daylight

Plumage (PLOO maj)—the covering of feathers on a bird

Predator (PRED a tor)—an animal that kills another animal for food

Prey (PRAY)—animals which are hunted for food by another animal

Species (SPEE sheez)—within a group of closely-related animals, such as owls, one certain kind or type

Talons (TAL ons)—long, hooked claws on the feet of birds

INDEX